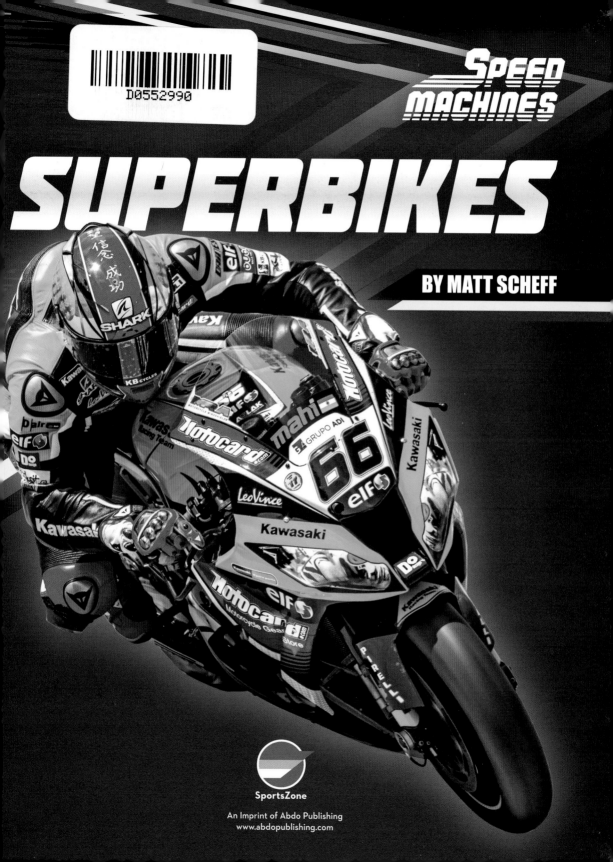

SPEED MACHINES

SUPERBIKES

BY MATT SCHEFF

SportsZone
An Imprint of Abdo Publishing
www.abdopublishing.com

D0552990

www.abdopublishing.com

Published by Abdo Publishing, a division of ABDO, PO Box 398166,
Minneapolis, Minnesota 55439. Copyright © 2015 by Abdo Consulting Group,
Inc. International copyrights reserved in all countries. No part of this
book may be reproduced in any form without written permission from the
publisher. SportsZone™ is a trademark and logo of Abdo Publishing.

Printed in the United States of America, North Mankato, Minnesota
092014
012015

 THIS BOOK CONTAINS
RECYCLED MATERIALS

Cover Photo: David Acosta Allely/Shutterstock Images
Interior Photos: David Acosta Allely/Shutterstock Images, 1; Mark Almond/
The Birmingham News/AP Images, 4-5; Mark Almond/AL.com/AP Images, 6-7;
Martin Cleaver/AP Images, 8-9, 12-13, 27; Rudi Brandstaetter/AP Images, 10-11;
Gurinder Osan/AP Images, 13; Shutterstock Images, 14, 18-19; Ivan Sekretarev/
AP Images, 14-15, 16-17, 24-25; Fernando Bustamante/AP Images, 20-21; Press
Association/AP Images, 22-23, 31; Cal Sport Media/AP Images, 26-27, 28-29

Editor: Chrös McDougall
Series Designer: Nikki Farinella

Library of Congress Control Number: 2014944192

Cataloging-in-Publication Data
Scheff, Matt.
 Superbikes / Matt Scheff.
   p. cm. -- (Speed machines)
ISBN 978-1-62403-615-6 (lib. bdg.)
Includes bibliographical references and index.
1. Superbikes--Juvenile literature.   I. Title.
629.227--dc23

                                                    2014944192

CONTENTS

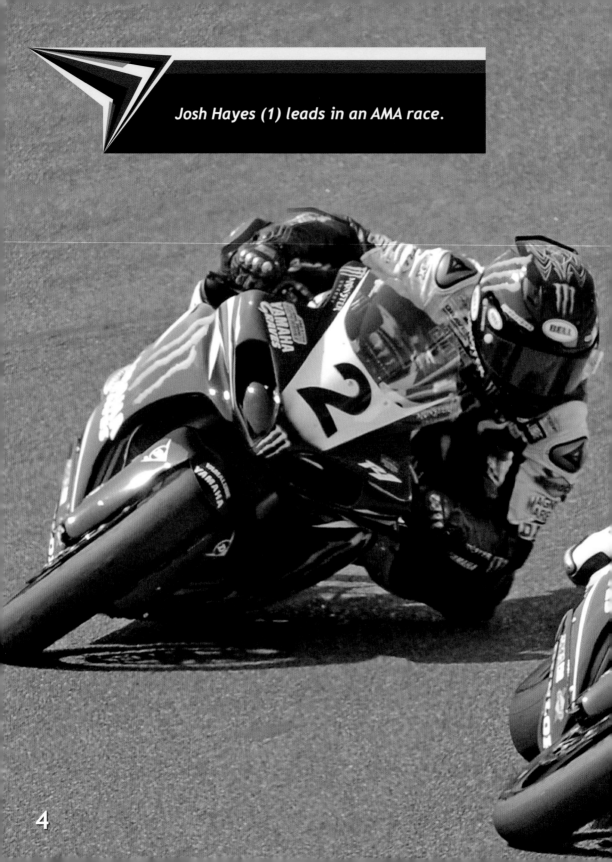

Josh Hayes (1) leads in an AMA race.

BY INCHES

It's a three-person race. Josh Hayes is leading the first race of the 2014 American Motorcyclist Association (AMA) Pro Superbike season. But Cameron Beaubier and Roger Hayden are close behind. Beaubier's engine roars as he pulls alongside Hayes. Beaubier gains ground, inch by inch. His bike's nose edges out to the lead.

Josh Hayes is one of the world's best superbike racers.

Beaubier comes into the next turn too fast. His superbike drifts to the top of the track. Now it's a two-person race. Hayden's bike screams down a straightaway. He pulls up alongside Hayes. The finish line is in sight. Hayden's bike rockets down the track. But Hayes has the inside line. Hayden can't hold the lead. The crowd cheers as Hayes crosses the finish line, winning by inches.

THE HISTORY OF SUPERBIKES

Ever since the motorcycle was invented in the late 1800s, riders have dreamed of speed. Soon, a class of motorcycles called sport bikes emerged. Sport bikes were built to maximize speed. But their low gas mileage meant they were not always practical. Honda introduced the CB750 in 1969. This bike combined top performance with features that improved the ride for everyday drivers. It was the first superbike.

FAST FACT

The CB750 topped out at 124 miles per hour (200 km/h). No other motorcycle on the road could match it.

A superbike racer in 1997

Some motorcycles are designed specifically for racing. Not superbikes. They are great for racing, but they're actually production motorcycles. A production motorcycle is an everyday bike that riders use on public streets. Superbikes take these bikes to a new level of speed and performance, though. These bikes were used mostly for racing early on. Their popularity exploded among regular riders during the 1970s and 1980s. Fans loved to own the same bikes driven by their favorite racers.

Superbike racing star Carl Fogarty leads a race in 1995.

Superbikes kept getting bigger and faster. In 1984, Kawasaki introduced the GPZ900R. This new bike had an engine cooled by liquid instead of air. In 1992, the Honda FireBlade set the standard for superbikes with its powerful engine and lightweight materials. In 1999, the Suzuki Hayabusa was the fastest superbike. It maxed out at 194 miles per hour (312 km/h).

FAST FACT

The Hayabusa is named for a type of falcon that can dive at 200 miles per hour (322 km/h).

A Suzuki Hayabusa in 2008

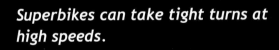

Superbikes can take tight turns at high speeds.

Superbikes race at a 2012 event in Russia.

PARTS OF A SUPERBIKE

Superbikes are like regular motorcycles that manufacturers modify for maximum speed. The chassis and body are super lightweight. The wheelbase is compact. This means that the front and back wheels are close together. A compact wheelbase makes a superbike easy to turn at high speeds.

Tom Sykes cruises along in a 2012 race.

The heart of a superbike is its engine. Modern superbikes have an inline-four engine. This type of engine has four fuel-burning cylinders arranged in a straight line. Racing-class superbikes burn a special high-octane fuel.

FAST FACT

A superbike engine can produce 170 horsepower or more. That's more than many full-sized cars.

FAST FACT

By 2000, superbikes were getting dangerously fast. So motorcycle manufacturers decided to voluntarily limit the power of future bikes.

Superbikes built for racing have special tires. Superbikes use soft, smooth tires called slicks. Slicks give the best possible grip on paved tracks. They can hug the track even during high-speed turns. But slicks also wear out quickly. During long races, racers must make pit stops to change the tires.

A superbike takes a tight turn.

Racing at high speeds is dangerous. Superbikes don't offer a lot of protection. So racers wear safety gear to protect them during crashes. They wear strong helmets with full-face visors. Many wear plates of strong, lightweight Kevlar over their chests. They cover this with racing leathers that protect the skin during crashes.

FAST FACT

The strong fabric Kevlar is also used to make bulletproof vests.

A rider loses control of his superbike during a 2008 race.

PHOTO DIAGRAM

1. front wheel

2. disc brakes

3. handlebars

4. helmet

5. body panels

6. riding leathers

7. chassis

8. fork exhaust

9. back wheel

SUPERBIKES IN ACTION

People around the world love riding their superbikes. They enjoy the raw speed and agility that these bikes provide. For some, nothing beats riding a powerful machine down the open road. For others, it's all about racing. Superbike racing series take place all over the world. The Superbike World Championship (SBK) is the main international series. The series is hosted around the world.

Racers take a turn in a superbike race.

FAST FACT

Carl Fogarty, riding Ducati motorcycles, won four SBK titles during the 1990s. That's the most in SBK history.

A rider takes a tight turn during a qualifying session.

SBK events begin with qualifying. Riders use a practice session and a qualifying round to get their fastest times. The top riders move on to a final qualifying session. There, the fastest rider earns the pole position. The remaining racers line up based on their times.

Carl Fogarty celebrates after winning a race in 1997.

In 1991, Doug Polen and his Ducati 888 won an amazing 17 out of 26 SBK races. He finished second in four more.

The race begins with a series of lights. When the final light goes out, the race is on! Racers battle for positions on the track. They drive into pit lane for fresh tires and repairs. Most races last about 100 kilometers (62 miles). Each of the top 15 finishers earns points toward the season championship. The racer with the most points at the end of the season is the winner.

Riders battle for position in a 2014 race.

GLOSSARY

chassis
The main frame of a vehicle.

Kevlar
The brand name for the high-strength fiber that makes up the chest protectors worn by motorcycle racers.

modify
To change a vehicle to make it more suitable for another purpose.

octane
A measure of the amount of a chemical in gasoline; high-octane fuels usually provide more power than low-octane fuels.

pit stop
Part of a race in which a driver drives the superbike off of the track and into the pit area to get fresh tires, fuel, adjustments, or all three.

pole position
The first starting position.

production motorcycle
A motorcycle built to be sold to the public, rather than built just for racing.

racing leathers
Protective leather clothing worn by motorcycle racers.

slicks
A smooth, soft type of tire used on superbikes and race cars.

wheelbase
The distance between the front and rear wheel of a motorcycle.

FOR MORE INFORMATION

Books
Harrison, Paul. *Superbikes*. Mankato, MN: Black Rabbit Books, 2013.

Ruck, Colleen. *Motorcycles*. Mankato, MN: Smart Apple Media, 2012.

Tieck, Sarah. *Superbikes*. Edina, MN: Abdo Publishing Co., 2011.

Websites
To learn more about Speed Machines, visit **booklinks.abdopublishing.com**. These links are routinely monitored and updated to provide the most current information available.

INDEX

ABOUT THE AUTHOR

Matt Scheff is a freelance author and lifelong motor sports fan living in Minnesota.